First-Hand Accounts from Made-up Places

Poems by Mike James

Stubborn Mule Press
Devil's Elbow, MO
stubbornmulepress@gmail.com

Copyright (c) Mike James, 2018
First Edition 1 3 5 7 9 10 8 6 4 2
ISBN: 978-1-946642-84-4
LCCN: 2018962902

Design, edits and layout: Jeanette Powers
Cover and title page image: Jon Lee Grafton
Author photo: Diane James
All rights reserved. No part of this publication may be reproduced or transmitted in any form or by any means, electronic or mechanical, including photocopying, recording or by info retrieval system, without prior written permission from the author.

Some of these poems have appeared, often in different versions, in the following magazines: *Gargoyle, As It Ought To Be, Visions International, Trailer Park Quarterly, Vox Populi, Mad Swirl, Rye Whiskey Review, Ekphrastic Review, Good Works Review, The Cape Rock,* and *Gasconade Review.*

No book is written in a vacuum.

The author would like to acknowledge the many people who read or listened to these poems and provided helpful feedback. Some of those fine folks include: Joan Colby, Scott Silsbe, Christopher Harter, Chase Dimock, Daniel Crocker, Larry Smith, John Dorsey, Jason Baldinger, and Jeff Alfier.

CONTENTS

I.

"Give me a wash cloth" / 1

"I threw my books in" / 2

"Old Robert Bly, white sharpness" / 3

"My wife tells me, her" / 4

"Something we learn, quickly, is" / 5

"There are two keys to" / 6

"Some words are heavy, filled" / 7

"This morning, I washed one" / 8

"The invention of the alarm" / 9

"If magic was real we" / 10

"This starless night, my country" / 11

"A garden doesn't make you" / 12

"When the rattlesnake lies on" / 13

"Those days when you suspect" / 14

"Noah gathered animals two by" / 15

"In songwriting, a hook is" / 16

"I plan to make a" / 17

"There's a bird singing beneath" / 18

"Here we are with an" / 19

"I go out looking for" / 20

"I'm waiting for the apocalypse" / 21

"At first, Ishmael went in" / 22

"We make a fetish of" / 23

"Prayers for every statistician in" / 24

"He spent his days in" / 25

II.

DIY / 27

Pittsburgh Ghazal / 28

Spring Turning / 29

Parson Weems' Fable / 30

Self-Portrait, 1932 / 31

American Gothic / 32

III.

Snow Angels in July / 34

Getting Up From the Couch / 35

My Investments / 36

Piñata Bombs / 37

The Chicken Riddle / 38

The Kingdom of Fake Beards / 39

Communique / 40

Stalin's Icepick / 41

Paul Lynde / 42

James Harvey, a Footnote / 43

Steve's Frowns / 44

Hairy Blanket / 45

Truman Capote's Twin Brother / 46

This One Songwriter / 47

On Freudian Slippers / 48

On Orgasm / 49

On Hedonism / 50

On Cuckoldry / 51

On Loss / 52

On Eyelashes / 53

On Finishing a Love Poem / 54

On Flip Flops / 55

On the Popsicle / 56

On Love Affairs, Break Ups, & Such / 57

For Joan Colby

I.

Americanized Ghazals

Give me a wash cloth and I will find a river to
dip it in. I will bathe in memory and in loss.

Whenever the sky seems bluer than the river,
remember, you only swim towards dirt.

I can't tell you all the places I've been.
Memory holds less geography, more loss.

Here's a wish for a young me…Don't be so
serious…Swim in the communion cup.
Curse in your prayers.

This poem might be less useful than a dirty joke.
There may be less wisdom, fewer good images.

I am afraid of all exit signs. Though I love any
abandoned factory, house or ghost town. Almost
every broken window.

An exit sign offers one way out. Just like the
river. A broken window might lead to an alley,
to another dark room.

I threw my books in the river.
Called myself a fool. Went for a swim.

The river only knows one direction to go.
So, I'm saying the river is like General Grant.

There are more than two sides to the river.
The fish know this. So do the birds.

At night, the river sounds like someone weeping.
Maybe because it's always going away.

If your heart breaks more than once a week,
go to the river. It's always saying yes.

Old Robert Bly, white sharpness gone from his teeth,
means just one thing when he says *it is late.*

My father told a story about breaking horses, born wild.
I could tell the story, but it's so damned late.

We can curse in our best Saturday night voice. Sing the
oldest Presbyterian hymns. It doesn't matter. It's too late.

Build a fire at night. Burn every want. Dance
as long as you wish. Do it all. Still, it's late.

If you believe in the worlds of *is* and *isn't,*
quit worrying. That coin's tossed. It's already late.

I know a good monk, his long road of weed, gravel, a
search for right. He tells me now, it's awfully late.

Those who play the lottery live on faith.
For those who live on water and salt…It's too late.

My wife tells me, her story is not my story. Then
she tells me, everyone has the same story. Again
and again, she's right.

I keep asking who I am. Wannabe teacher. Failed rodeo
rider. Twice suppressed drag queen. My broken Magic
Eight Ball won't answer.

Most days start without making a wish. I've only got so
many in my wish jar. So I'm cautious. Keep them at my
bedside. Treasure them like half-dollars.

Whenever I earn money, it's already spent! That's why
my wish jar is so important. For *bucket list* items,
lottery tickets, and discontinued love notes.

Don't laugh, but my favorite way to go is up. That's
practice for heaven. If I go backwards, down too far, I
only find the empty shell that's my heart.

Something we learn, quickly, is who comes when we call. We learn this before we learn color, before we know blue.

Need has a color. Think of red. Throw a dart…Land on lust. That's why dart boards are in bars! Lust lists change. We learn all our colors.

One of the things a child might ask, as children ask and ask, is what shapes the rain. Gravity is one answer. Rain's desire for dirt, another.

You know what a soldier learns, after how to hold a gun? Every open grave waits to be filled. The rain knows this too, in a different way.

There are a thousand quotes about the rain. The rain remembers only a few. Yesterday tries to tell something. We forget who yesterday was.

There are two keys to my house. That's one too many.
Maybe I'll give away both keys and the red front door.

I crawl through windows to practice my thievery.
I watch for broken glass, moonlight shards, graffiti
droppings.

Deep night is almost pornographic. Not all lamp post
shadow puppets resemble rabbits, dogs, and ducks.

The best way out of darkness is boredom. That's a quote
direct from *Reader's Digest*. If you condense wisdom,
it loses teeth.

I never had trouble with my teeth until I was forty.
Maybe our teeth exit first, make a path for our bodies.

Some words are heavy, filled with slow sadness, as if each
is a stone lifted from the pocket of the river.

Sometimes, we search hard for an epiphany. Lift up
every green, mossy rock. Sometimes, guess what, there's
not one!

As a child, I thought rain had a meaning. Later,
I learned rain has many lovers. Gravity among them.

Once upon a time, I focused on the oyster's bit of sand.
Now, I think of the lucky pebble in my old coat pocket.

My grandmother, fishing pole in hand, said I talked
the fish away. She believed fish, the best listeners, knew
words by their ripples.

I have few beliefs. Words are vines that cover them.
Grace is just dew that gathers in honeysuckle an hour
before daylight.

This morning, I washed one week's worth of dirty dishes
in the bathtub. Then lined them up in my driveway to dry.

The mailman only delivers envelopes from the past.
Trained pigeons occupy my front porch. Also, at night,
I dream about movie Nazis.

My favorite recipes involve celery and abundant tears.
Friends sound off like angry geese at my cooking. All
potluck invitations go amiss.

As a child, I struggled to learn my left from my right. Now,
I mainly point for my wants. Use a vocabulary of one-sided
grunts. A chipmunk imitating a bear.

Next week I'm planning a road trip to the edge of
something. Maybe a crisis. Maybe a canyon. Maybe a plain,
American ditch.

The invention of the alarm clock depressed roosters, worldwide. Still, they strut and strut. Much more than crows with their long patience.

I repeat myself in order to remember the few things I know. Often, I sound like a whip-poor-will listing off night's many purposes.

Last week I learned two new things. One involved the love life of ostriches. The other was the secret behind silky red bow ties.

Some weeks I learn nothing new. I'm just a crow in the sun, sitting on a power line, waiting and waiting for summer.

Did I mention that I repeat myself? I wish I had one line I could repeat in all my poems. I'd like the line to end with flamingos.

If magic was real we would all disappear. Not just our
problems. Quicker than a meteor in a dinosaur's wink,
we'd be gone, gone.

If I was going to die in the saddle, I'd buy new boots.
Shiny black ones. Silver spurs. Everyone could hear me
jangling down the trail a last time.

So much of life is about going away. Pay the ferryman
for the use of his boat. Watch the water always on its way.

After Robert Johnson walked with the Devil, he left many
unrecorded songs. Among his greatest is *You Don't Know
Me, That's OK, I Already Left Blues.*

All these lines are vessels of joy. Even sad looking ones.
Joy's in the cracks. Mixed with the mud. Joy fires the kiln.

This starless night, my country back porch is the only
luminous thing for miles. From here you can hear an
owl ask and ask his one question.

The day she left I quit asking questions. Decided to
work to exhaustion. Burned every candle's both ends.
Shoveled ditches. Mended fences. Read Tolstoy end-to-end.

Even the cat is more sullen since she left. Named Sappho as
both homage and joke, she hides beneath the broken back
couch away from my rough, love-starved hands.

The young woman at the coffee shop…Either flirtatious or
just nice. I can't be sure. I stutter through small talk.
Think to quote her Milton. Decide not.

If Rumi were here, he'd tell me to go plow a field.
He'd phrase it with luminous grace, not in my sleep
exhausted way. He'd phrase it so it could be repeated
after many years.

A garden doesn't make you a farmer any more
than boots make you a cowboy. Go on and play
your make-believe. Go to your fashion show.

Appropriation is the least appreciated art. Going
forward, we should only speak in quotes from
Colette, Betty Boop, and her doe-eyed ilk.

If thievery was legal, where would the fun be?
Cat burglars no more romantic than postman.
Duchamp, another man with an extra urinal.

Listen, the whole world practices make-believe.
Have you ever seen a President give an oath with
fingers not crossed? That was a dream.

Matthew Broderick once parroted the line,
*There's a kind of freedom in being completely
screwed.* Let me an offer an agreement.
Give an amen.

When the rattlesnake lies on asphalt at night, her body stretched to exclamation, all she's looking for is warmth.

Even a dying star gives off light. You remember that fact from tenth grade science class, but you forget the formula for warmth.

Prophets in the desert bathed in ashes, wore unpainted sackcloth, ate locusts, and still gave hosannas. All in a longing for warmth.

Moses, when he turned his eyes away from the desert flaming bush, was frightened not by the sight or by the voice, but by the warmth.

At day's end, what do you fear? Not snakes. Not that night dream of being lost in the desert. Only a final darkness, past any ring of warmth.

Those days when you suspect Jimmy Buffett is a secret Buddha. His great loves of bed, table, and bottle, interludes between sufferings.

Some days we wait for something to happen. Invariably, it does. We look for words for our big events. Often, we use only vowels.

When looking for words, don't forget alphabet soup! Don't get so caught up in the letters you forget the broth's deliciousness.

What words do you find in alphabet soup? Like Freud, do you spell out *mother*? Like St. Francis, do you start with *thanks*?

A teacher once told me to never end a poem on a question. She was a specialist in suffering. Her thank you cards always tear sealed.

Noah gathered animals two by two. Desire works the same way. Not one person, alone. Like our hands, desire is a coupling.

Both is my favorite. That's a problem. Give me the cherry pie along with the apple. Give me the cheerleader and the pool boy.

My favorite place to go is inside my head. Pleasures and damnation swim along as old friends. Sometimes, it's like ice-skating in hell.

Sartre said *hell is other people.* My father said hell is where I'm going. Thankfully, Sartre is not my father. I live, helpless, among ambiguities.

The only thing I miss is what I leave out. For instance, there's no you in these lines. I know…Cue violins. Maybe brass trumpets. A kazoo.

In songwriting, a hook is the line which grabs a listener's attention. I want hooks that cut deep as Jim Bowie's knife, while I remember the Alamo.

So many of us run away from pain. We put on our track shoes. Stretch. Then it's ready-set-go. We are off! Chasing after that blue bird bliss.

Something I found out today…comfort food has limits. Banana pudding only dampens anxiety. Fried chicken won't polish a tattooed heart.

Some folks love the rain because the rain seems to weep and weep. Who doesn't love the person who can spend days drowning, three feet off-shore?

Of course, like so many inland-born fools, I never learned to swim. I'm not even good at holding my breath. After a few seconds I look at the sky, give in.

I plan to make a pilgrimage to Buddy Ebsen's
well-regarded tomb. I'm going to wear overalls,
a straw hat. Drink from a jug? You bet.

My accent doesn't travel well. I tell people this is
how Shakespeare sounded, back in the day. They just
nickname me Jethro and laugh.

You know, Hollywood never gets southerners right.
Either sweet as a grandma's dimples or rawer than an
infected cut. Turtle slow, no matter.

The Phoenix was a southern bird. Assigned to ruination,
flames, and rebirth. In small towns referred to as
Gamecock. His sporting battles, strictly illegal.

I leave my compass when I leave the south. Kansas wind
sends me one way. Pittsburgh rain another. Until I'm on
a road edged with kudzu, I'm mostly lost.

There's a bird singing beneath the hood of my car.
Somewhere near the engine. I can walk to work.
I can call in sick today.

The birds above the sidewalk might be welcoming me
or one another. They also might be saying, *Look at that
clown with his fancy shoes!*

I wasn't made for the outdoors. My hands as small as the
hands of certain presidents. Feel free to insert joke.
Draw conclusions.

Just yesterday, a pigeon followed me home. Say what you
will about instinct or supposed pigeon intelligence.
That fellow was lost.

Tomorrow, as Scarlett O'Hara says, is another day.
It's my plan to wake up singing. If I'm out of tune…
Oh well. My bulldog, Fifi, will still chime in.

Here we are with an empty sky. Stars don't appear despite our need for a wish. Our imagination can operate from counterfeit options.

Bukowski's gravesite advice is right...*Don't try*. Let things happen. Just wait. Some puzzles were meant to be left in a box.

Here are two simple wants. Neither involves money or sex. One is to know the name of each person on my street. The second is not to blush so easily.

If I went away I'd grow a beard. People would recognize me by my facial hair. They might call me farmer then comment on my smooth, white sculpted hands.

The day I moved into my house no neighbor came over to greet me. Movers left. Night started early and dark. Clouds even gave the moon something else to do.

I go out looking for wisdom. Mainly find humor.
In misdirected fortune cookies. In graffiti. A hound dog
distracted by any scent. Whatever I land on is by chance.

Parts of reality need to be refuted. The way gravity
works, eventually, on all of us. Yes, balloon animals too.
Even eagles have to descend.

I must have been a bird in a past life. Once, an old
love told me that. Nothing unpronounceable, exotic.
A hummingbird, beating his heart out for a few seasons.

In my next life, I plan to raise pet opossums. That's not
a thing now, but I'm planning on the future when all pets
will need a garbage smile.

An opossum doesn't divide the world into trash and
treasure. It's all treasure. Thanks for the fig tree's sweet
feast. Thanks for the trashcan left open.

I'm waiting for the apocalypse or the rapture. In the meantime, I'm reading Stein. Also, growing cabbages and watching John Wayne movies while I paint my nails.

Some people pretend to live without shadows. Are always perfectly shaved. Ignore salsa stains, flatulence. Expect worry to be, at least, three houses away.

The best we hope for are angels grown tired of heaven's many perfections. Who miss beer, sex, mascara. Who miss a world happy to wake from dreams.

On slow days, I work in the garden. The squirrels seem to like what I produce. In good years I harvest peppers, cucumbers. Bad years, profanity and (yep) dust.

Art News tells us, second chances are no harder than the first. We just write songs about the second. We romanticize failure since we all have practice.

At first, Ishmael went in search of a ship. Later, a coffin.
That's so often the order of things. Not even the fastest
sailboat outruns the destination.

You can build your own coffin. Shape the wood.
Decorate it with unicorn drawings, stickers of where
you've been. Ultimately, it's also for travel.

If you happen to build a coffin, shaped like a ship,
it doesn't mean you obsess over sailing or death.
Could just mean you knew a sailor, once, who made
an impression.

Every vessel is meant for travel. Even houseboats are
built to leave the shore. Stay too close to land and you
forget the feel of open wind.

Melville said, true places are never on a map. So…We are
all directionally challenged! True north might be open sky.
Those four points on a compass might not track to home.

We make a fetish of the possible. No one invests in time machines or jackalope farms. No one steps on a river and expects to walk away.

Away might be the best place to start. I'm a believer in starting points. That's part of Geometry, 101. Draw a line in any direction. It's still away.

When we say we angle for something, it means we want it. Might be just sympathy, handed over like a towel to dry up that first river called tears.

Tears also go away. Time and gravity certifies that.
Did Confucius say, our salt waters nothing? Let's say he did. Let's pretend wisdom.

I'd as soon plow a field as write a poem. That's not wisdom. It's a damned lie. I hate sweat, love laughter, and plant my poems in the ground, facing south.

Prayers for every statistician in love with mystery, that
valley beneath the mist. Pity for anyone allergic to all of it.

Religious language is, now and then, used for emphasis.
Throw a jawbone down when you smite someone.
Move verily, verily along.

You know, most mythologies are similar. The war gods
clash in common battles. The great flood has various,
peculiar names.

One thing I always ask for…Blessings. More practical than
wishes, less greed based. No miser's hand out for money.
Just a fern washed by rain.

If I were looking for a new Buddha, I would start with
a highway road crew. The best sign for transcendence is
Under Construction.

He spent his days in search of exultation. As for his nights...Fill in the blank with a headshake, a strong verb, a smile, or a wish.

He always gave money to panhandlers, especially if they were saving for a new tattoo. Skin provides an atlas. Directions always by hand.

For him, duty wasn't even an off-rhyme for pleasure. Duty was another language. Not an old one, like Latin. One made up to rhyme with guess.

Whiskey was constantly at hand. Not just for snake bites, also for nights. This is sentimental, but true...His smile would shake loose a wish.

Did I mention, *always* was a word he hated to use? Listen to a hundred stories, he'd never say it. He said always was a place he never knew.

II.

Interludes & Homages

DIY

The way you break my heart
just to play with glue.

Your hands all sticky
as you piece together
what was fine
before.

Each time,
it's a little different.

Almost always, there's
one piece
left on the floor.

Pittsburgh Ghazal

for Jason Baldinger

Michael (who's hard of hearing now) tells me,
You have to pay attention! I shut my eyes whenever
he drives. Try not to think about the next bridge.

Every time I cross a bridge, there's a tunnel attached.
That's probably all in my head. You know, I brake when I
see the tunnel's light? I want to stay here.

One of the things I'm most attached to is place. I love
more than one river. I even like slow traffic. It lets me
watch two rivers merge when light's clear.

The rivers appear in poem after poem. They gather
runoff, lovers, and surprises. They gather old men beside
them and pigeons who learn voices if not names.

No bar I go to is ever snow closed. All the owners are
old, tough and make that clear. The rivers go their one
way in heat or cold.

Every bridge was built before I was born.

Spring Turning
after Grant Wood

In a green evening a man fell asleep
and dreamed himself
into the bright and shallow colors
of a field.

A valley formed along the back of his thighs.
The grass grew cooler there.

In his deep slumber the hills remained.

Two farmers came from different ways
and staked their claims.

They fenced the fields
and tilled the soil, so richly new.

And when they saw one another,
behind horse and plow,
they waved across all that was there.

Parson Weems' Fable
after Grant Wood

Though he knew, already, how to hold
an axe handle and knew, too,
those many farm uses,
there was never a front yard cherry tree.

Nothing waited to be cleaved by
young George's boredom.

But this is an old story
and, like so many of the best,
not bound by the day-to-day
dreariness of facts.

Notice the curtain, though.
one hand holds it back while
the other centers
our gaze directly.

The tree, split but not
all the way.

The axe, matched in brightness
to the father's coat.

George's face already like a dollar bill.
his tights bluer than background sky.

Self-Portrait, 1932
after Grant Wood

That face in fear of smiles
or recognition.

The sunburn hides a permanent blush
and the forehead's slope
almost matches
the soft slant of background hills.

As for the eyes,
the glasses don't hide their
sideways glance.

Outside, the windmill is too still
to pull more color
out of the faded sky.

He loves no color more than the sun.

There's so much to not see
past the fields.

American Gothic

after Grant Wood

The man has given up. His tractor won't work.
His old, shaggy brown horse, half-lame,
long ready for that last field to cross.

The woman has forgotten every
feeling except disappointment.
The brooch she wears, firm at her neck,
the last of her mother's fine things.

Their marriage started as a snicker among
neighbors. Never changed.
The woman hoped, just once, for a fairy tale.
The man, even in the bathtub, smelled of the farm.

On the wrong day, that pitchfork might be a weapon.
The Gothic window, though church-like,
never points toward grace.

III.

Visitations
Prose Poems

Snow Angels in July

As a boy, I could never decide between Captain America's shield and Wonder Woman's golden lasso. Childhood's hardest decision was normally settled by the toss of a two-headed coin. If that sounds absurd, you should meet my wife. And if you think she's too absurd, you should meet her wife. It all goes from there. I'm like Sisyphus as a Candy Man pushing a giant ball of sugar uphill. Every ant I come across wants a piece of the day's work. I spend hours and hours worried about the chance of rain, despite what the best weathermen say. I can't remember when it wasn't like this. The mailman drops off a daily package of rose colored threats. He smells like autumn and out-of-date aftershave. Neighbors shout at him, in Albanian, through lace curtains. At night, the Bat-Signal shines against the sky. Bruce Wayne is secretly a crank. He hates orphans and the letter Q. I met him once, at a party, Catwoman on his arm. She was dressed in her tired black leather. Every man and woman kept tripping to hand her saucer after saucer of cream.

Getting Up From the Couch

My doctor said I need exercise. You can guess why.
Fat genes and cookies go together like chocolate and
peanut butter. So, I decided to go swim in my television.
The water was the perfect temperature. Trouble was…
I couldn't see the bottom…All those crazy wires and
leftover game show prizes. Every few minutes a mermaid
brushed past my legs. Her long hair tickled my toes.
I've never cared much for fish, but that was nice.
Oh, that was real nice.

My Investments

Not one pharmacist in town will trade an aspirin for a haiku. The butcher shakes her head when I offer a rhyme (internal or end) for a sausage or a pork chop. Her eyes seem sad when she turns away. The dry cleaner says, *Stay away with your damned alliteration. Poetry won't pay for permanent press.* Vending machines shut down when I walk past. No change jingles in my loose pockets. At the bus stop, a man moves down a few seats when I ask if he needs an erasure epic. Even the little girl at the lemonade stand shoos me away with both hands. Only dollars will bring a new bike. Especially one with glittered streamers which catch the downhill wind.

Piñata Bombs

The enemy never expected piñatas to darken noon. They came down, bright as happy memories, across all the small country. Each attached to a parachute no bigger than two handkerchiefs together.

When people saw the piñatas they froze, fingers pointing, mouths shaped to the letter O. Then, everyone grabbed the nearest broom.

Some piñatas were filled with counterfeit chocolate coins. Others with bright gumballs and chewing gum. A few contained only an excess of silvery glitter. More than one held a single, calligraphic note of…*Sorry, Try Again.*

Most of the piñatas not battered open were adopted and became house piñatas. The few not adopted were shipped off to a piñata farm where a famous general once lived.

The Chicken Riddle

All day a chicken sits on one side of the road dreaming of the other side. Cars move quickly down the road. No one slows down for a solitary, white chicken.

It's a busy road. A busy day. People have lives to live. Cars have services to provide before they break down or get traded. The chicken sits and sits.

She imagines the sun as a giant egg. She imagines clouds as giant eggs. She cannot dream herself to flight. So, back she goes to the barnyard and the clucks of her sisters.

On nights when the moon is full and the sky especially bright and clear, she sneaks from her coop and into the garden and imagines every row of tomatoes a dirt road that even her shadow can cross.

The Kingdom of Fake Beards

Began with abundance. After the problems of hunger, education, war, and owl blindness were solved and psychoanalysis proved effective for every middle-aged child and scientists made multi-colored pills so gender or race could change as easily as shoes (so combat boots one day, six inch stilettos the next), after those things came to be, citizens refused boredom. Thankfully, there were fake beards. First worn by coffee shop prophets, then by kindergarteners, then by politicians (who thought they looked smarter and, so, acted that way), and then by checkout girls. That's when the fun really started. Some went full pirate, decorated their locks with tassels and ribbons. Others donned shaded or glittery goatees. A happy few could pull off the Van Dyke in spring time. The white curls of Santa were fashionable year round.

Communique

for Chase Dimock

Bosnian snipers are everywhere. Especially in the wheat fields outside of Omaha. They send obscene postcards to the local police department and to the many chapters of the DAR. They make prank phone calls, in southern accents, to retirement homes for Union soldiers. Almost every bridge underpass is riddled with their secret graffiti, so easily translated with a basic decoder ring. Some graffiti give directions to heaven. Others, only directions to home.

Stalin's Icepick

The first time Stalin saw Trotsky, he was struck by the way he held a teacup. The way his fingers seemed to gather warmth in the open cathedrals that were his hands. He wondered if Trotsky's goatee ever bathed in milk, if his eyes ever slowed from dancing.

Stalin often thought of Trotsky at night. He would smoke his pipe and play with his favorite icepick, the one with a handle engraved with a fist holding a flower with a small bee in the center.

There was nothing Stalin would trade for his icepick. Not for one of Blok's poems. Not for the scent of gooseberries. Not for an extra sunlit hour. Not even for sheep milk, served in a teacup, sweetened with honey.

Paul Lynde

Died on an early January Sunday in Beverly Hills. If he'd
been born in early January, he'd be a Capricorn. He was
a Gemini. During the 1970's it was popular to tell people
your sign. Like shag carpet, that's less popular now.
Paul trusted astrology. Call him a man of the times.
Call him Liberace without a piano, add a scarf. Geminis
love illusions and music. Prefer light blue and yellow.
The great talents of Geminis *are in the social realm.*
Does that include cooking? Paul Lynde liked to drink
white wine while cooking. He loved to cook.

James Harvey, a Footnote

Warhol liked the look of Brillo Pad boxes. Liked them on grocery store shelves and in end-of-the-aisle stacks. Liked the shine of clean lettering, just as he liked light off white linoleum.

James Harvey designed the Brillo Pad boxes. He did it for a check, etc. Away from the office, Harvey painted colored abstracts. An *action painter* who wore a tie.

Warhol made wooden sculptures of Brillo Pad boxes. Warhol borrowed / lifted / used / stole / appropriated / purloined / liberated / pilfered / adapted / refashioned / transformed / adjusted / amended /and habituated himself with James Harvey's design.

Warhol used his own ideas when he was dying his eyebrows. That took a while. And the Brillo Pad boxes were there to be copied. They sat on a shelf and no one noticed they were art until he said so. He spoke very quietly. You had to lean in to hear.

Steve's Frowns

If he listed a few of his favorite things, frowning would be one. Some thought his face defaulted to a frown. Others thought he only frowned. He had a weekday frown and a Saturday frown. He had a first, second, third, fourth, and fifth Sunday frown. He had a frown for leap years. And frowns for the holidays: Christmas and Arbor Day, Fourth of July and John Denver's Birthday. At night, he counted frowns instead of sheep. As an insomniac since the age of two he might count into thousands, sometimes until daylight filled the whole room.

Hairy Blanket

Linda was a sorceress, not a witch. As with *average* and *mediocre,* there's a difference. She met Jeff when he was a black bear, in deep autumn. Linda loved the width of his stance and the swell of his paunch and the way he foraged for every bit of honey.

With a very small spell, Linda changed Jeff into her wish. It didn't take much. Even her beloved conjunctions held magic enough.

Taking him to her house, she shaved his chest and back. Then his arms. Then his butt, which took a while. Then his legs and feet. When she was done, he was large and pink and rounded, with no edges at all, and far from ordinary since no man who was once a bear can ever be ordinary.

With only her hands and no hint of a spell, Linda made a blanket of hair. When she unfurled it in the bedroom it covered the bed, the lamp, the dresser, the antique chest, and the unclouded mirror. And it covered her and Jeff. The blanket was warm. Even on the coldest nights, they couldn't see their breath.

Truman Capote's Twin Brother

Not that Truman Capote. Not the novelist and *bon vivant*. No, Truman Capote, the burly owner of an engine repair shop whose mother loved to read. His twin brother, Lionel Capote, named after a sailor the mother loved from wishful distance.

Truman could fix any engine, large or small. Lionel couldn't fix toast. He could make a screen door not work. He gave wrenches bad habits. Appliances became listless around him. These aren't jokes. They are truisms. Lionel wasn't small or fey. He was awkwardly large and awkwardly slow.

Truman fixed whatever people brought and he fixed quick. Lionel sat and watched and smoked and only spoke now and again. He stared at each engine as if every part of the engine might make a wound. Beneath the wounds were wildflowers.

This One Songwriter

Centered his work on obscurity. There was the song about James Buchanan's love life. And the one about Candy Darling's passion for limburger cheese. There was the one his mother liked about the many purposes of Mr. Spock's ears. And his own favorite about the woman he took out for coffee who left while he was pouring sugar.

Sometimes he forgot the lyrics and just hummed as he picked and poked at his taped up guitar. He was never very good at guitar tuning. Easily distracted, he often imagined guitar strings as Rapunzel's golden hair.

On Freudian Slippers

My mother never liked slippers. My father wore them everywhere, despite her protests. The office women all knew the wispy sound his tassels made when he walked angrily down the hall to yell about butterfly migrations and Peruvian milk shares. The tassels looked like dandelions. They swayed, but did not scatter.

Those were periwinkle ones, just for work. At home, we all knew we were in trouble the moment he put his hummingbird slippers on.

On Orgasm

The orgasm can't spell and has no concerns of that.
Also, lives on hunger and light. Counts in seconds
and shudders. Has a vocal range which begins many
basements down and finishes somewhere above bird flight.

Is tremulous a favorite word? Hardly. Orgasm is seldom
twinned. Not like a pear's two pitted halves. Though the
orgasm can be like slicing.

On Hedonism

Desire is an easy chair. A place to rest in the hunger of yes. One of the things my legs can do is *wrap around*. There's a blank after wrap around that can be filled in or erased. It's this way year round, especially in spring. As whoever dances alone hears music a different way. Emptiness is never like rapture.

On Cuckoldry

The cuckoo moves headfirst into other's nests.
She cannot help herself. So there's a metaphor. Take it as
relief. As relief comes, some nights, through the leash of
your sweat. Yeah, like that. That joy you take gazing at
skin marked with another's address. Repetition can turn
almost any noise into song.

On Loss

Things go away. Your mother told you that, first. Then your wife. Your mother meant headaches, allergies…Small nuisances. Your wife meant people. Only people. The door marked EXIT exists only for people to walk through.

A friend's long hair always made you think of a field in Africa, a place you never visited. The coupling never made sense, but never stopped happening. Some nights you crouched in the tall grass. Other nights you ran and ran.

On Eyelashes

They are for signaling hello and goodbye and come here and when you come here do it languidly, with an anticipatory smile. Some put big fake ones on which is even more languidness and anticipation, more hellos and goodbyes.

They are for the mirror and the hours and hours in front of it. The eyes are the cities. They are the suburbs. The mirror can tell when the soul packs up and moves there.

On Finishing a Love Poem

Once the last line is written, last comma placed, once every *and* is replaced with an &, and all the names changed from real to mythical, and all gender pronouns come to agree, remember to lean nose close to the paper and with damp, salt addicted tongue lick every corner of the page.

On Flip Flops

We hear what is coming, but stay in place to see. It's like the Godzilla movies where everyone stops to watch, but no fiery monsters will be killed today. Not for the sound that is mainly summer and often the beach. The one that encourages downward gazing. That favorite sound of feet fetishists. Also the sound that reminds miserly, penny hoarders to check their ground.

On the Popsicle

Don't sound too sexually provocative. That's hard when it involves an object which exists only to be licked or sucked for a sugar rush of mouth staining pleasure.

We can go back to childhood. Children, the main proprietors of this treat. They hold them in clutched fingers with the single purpose they give to the smallest things. That image is pure. It is like Norman Rockwell painting in summer sunlight on a weekday in the park.

Popsicle is a trademark. There's nothing sexy about trademarks. Kleenex is also a trademark. Kleenex never sounds provocative. Not even for teenage boys and lonely, hotel room men.

A popsicle left on a park bench melts in the summer heat with a slow drip which stains the bench and the world. After a short while there's nothing left but the stick. Then it's no longer a popsicle. It is once again a tongue depressor or a tiny piece of lumber for whatever squirrels or birds want to build.

On Love Affairs, Break Ups, & Such

Heart plus flowers equals a drug store valentine.
Open the card. There's a door inside. Behind the door,
a tunnel goes down farther than light shows. Don't be
afraid of the dark. Tell yourself that again and again,
like an old man in an ancient church saying thankless
prayers. Go on in. Delight in the cold. Your hunger
comes in waves, directed by the moon. It ebbs and flows.

Mike James has been widely published in magazines, large and small, throughout the country. His eleven previous poetry collections include: *Crows in the Jukebox* (Bottom Dog), *My Favorite Houseguest* (FutureCycle), and *Peddler's Blues* (Main Street Rag). He has served as an associate editor for the *Kentucky Review* and Autumn House Press, as well as the publisher of the now defunct Yellow Pepper Press. He makes his home outside Nashville, Tennessee. More info at: mike.jamespoetry.com

www.ingramcontent.com/pod-product-compliance
Lightning Source LLC
Chambersburg PA
CBHW030132100526
44591CB00009B/616